Body Maintenance

Contents

Teeth

When you were born, you had no teeth. Your first teeth started to grow when you were about six months old. They are called milk teeth. At the age of about six your permanent teeth begin to grow. They push the milk teeth out. Your four wisdom teeth do not arrive until you are an adult.

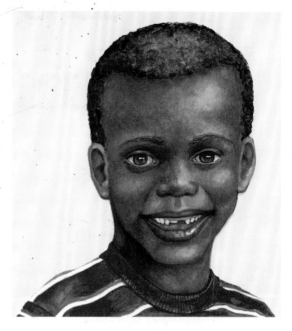

Diagram that shows what is inside a tooth

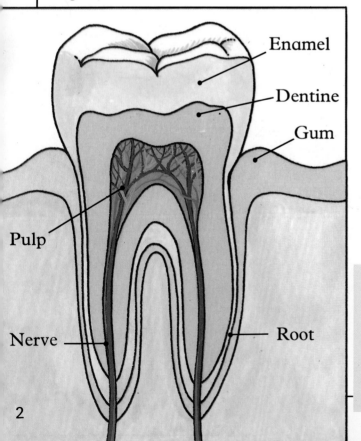

Enamel

Dentine

Gum

Pulp

Nerve

Root

Each tooth has a **root** which fixes it into your jaw. The top layer of the tooth is white. It is called **enamel**. It is very hard. **Dentine** is a softer layer underneath. The **pulp** inside the tooth contains nerves and blood vessels.

⭐ Enamel is the hardest part of your body. It is harder than a metal saucepan!

Jobs for teeth

Your teeth break up food in your mouth when you eat. They make the food ready to swallow.

Teeth have different shapes for different jobs.

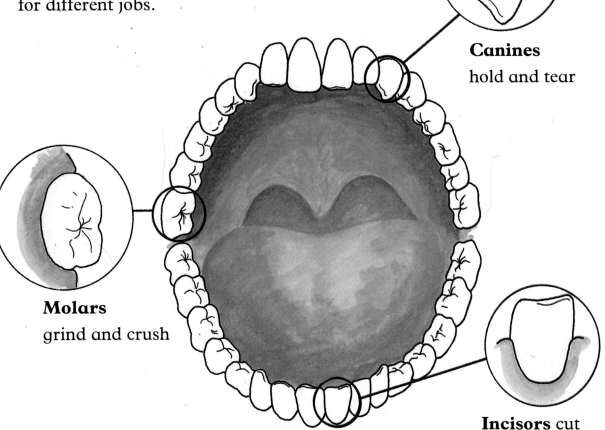

Canines hold and tear

Molars grind and crush

Incisors cut

Look after your permanent teeth. You will not grow any more!

 Can you make a model tooth out of plasticine?

Animals' teeth

Animals which eat one particular sort of food have special teeth. Rodents, like rabbits and guinea-pigs, have very long incisors. They eat vegetables which need to be cut and gnawed. Their teeth wear down, but they keep on growing. Sometimes the incisors grow too long. If we keep rodents as pets we must give them hard vegetables to eat. Otherwise the vet has to trim the long incisors. ⬇

★ The biggest teeth belong to the elephant. An elephant's tusk is a type of tooth. One African elephant's tusks measured three and a half metres long.

The teeth of cattle and goats continue to grow too. Cows eat lots of grass and their grinding teeth work all day long. ⬇

Dogs have big canine teeth. These sharp teeth are for tearing meat off bones. Dogs' teeth do not carry on growing. They stay clean and healthy by chewing on hard biscuits. ⬇

Rosemary's Teeth

Rosemary Freeth
had holes in her teeth,
deeper than ten metre rules.
So she said with a shout—
'Take all my teeth out
and I'll sell them for swimming pools.'

Michael Dugan

End of a Girl's First Tooth

Once she'd a tooth that wiggled;
Now she's a gap that lisps.
For weeks she could only suck lollies;
Now she champs peanuts and crithsps.

Roy Fuller

Going to the dentist

Andrew Skilbeck is a dentist in the Midlands. We asked him about caring for our teeth.

What do you do all day?

Andrew:
Dentists used to do a lot of drilling and filling. But I spend a lot of time helping people to look after their teeth.

Do all children have milk teeth?
Yes. Four-year-olds have 20 milk teeth; as many as all their fingers and toes! At six we grow four extra teeth. We must take care of milk teeth. They rot faster than adult teeth.

How do teeth rot?
A white fur collects on our teeth all the time. It would collect even if we ate nothing. This fur is called **plaque**. Harmful bacteria live in the plaque. They feed on sticky sugars and make acids.

What do the acids do?
The acids eat away our teeth, especially in the join between our teeth and our gums.

⭐ The crocodile bird looks after the crocodile's teeth. It picks out scraps of food from the crocodile's jaw.

How can we stop them?

By brushing our teeth regularly, especially after meals and before bed. Brushing before meals can help too. It removes the plaque before the sugars can get to work.

What should we use to brush our teeth?

We need a brush of the right size and fluoride toothpaste.

We all like sweets. Are they bad for teeth?

Sweets are bad for teeth. But so are cakes and sugary drinks. Even baked beans and tomato sauce have sugar in them.

Can't we eat sweets?

If you eat sweets, eat them all in one go, it will do less harm.

That sounds greedy.

Keeping sweets in your mouth feeds the bacteria for hours on end. Then they will do a lot more damage.

We are going to lose our milk teeth anyway. So why look after them?

Our milk teeth show our adult teeth where to grow. Without them, our adult teeth will not grow properly.

Can dentists help?

Yes. But you must visit your dentist at least twice a year. That way, he can catch troubles in time.

Thank you, Andrew.

We have to look after our teeth properly from the moment they first appear. Design and make a poster for five-year-olds to tell them how to look after their teeth. Make up five rules for sensible health care.

Smile, please

At one time, people in China liked yellow teeth. They stained them by eating herbs. Some warriors filed their teeth to points. In parts of Arabia, people thought that black teeth were beautiful. But nowadays most people prefer white teeth—and the best way to keep them white is to clean them every day.

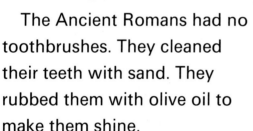

The Ancient Romans had no toothbrushes. They cleaned their teeth with sand. They rubbed them with olive oil to make them shine.

Years ago, in the jungles of Papua New Guinea and South America, people cleaned their teeth by chewing bark and sticks. In some parts of the world, people still use chewing-sticks today.

In Britain, 400 years ago, people cleaned their teeth with their fingers or with pieces of rough cloth. They used all kinds of things to make their teeth shine. Some people used salt. Others used cold ashes from the fire. Some even used breadcrusts or bacon fat.

William Addis invented the first toothbrush in 1780. He was a tanner; his job was making leather from animal skins. He stuck bristles in a wooden handle to make a toothbrush. He brushed his teeth with soap. The soap made his teeth gleam with cleanness. But it also made him foam at the mouth! His neighbours were terrified.

Some people still use toothbrushes made of wood and animal hair. But most modern toothbrushes are plastic. Few people nowadays brush their teeth with sand, bacon fat or soap. Instead, we use toothpaste from a tube. Chemicals in the toothpaste protect our teeth and a minty taste makes our mouths feel clean and fresh.

Laughing gas

About 200 years ago, Humphry Davy and his friend visited a fair. They watched jugglers, sword-swallowers and fire-eaters. They let Gipsy Lavengro tell their fortunes. They tried to guess the weight of the fattest man on earth.

It's the dentist! He's pulling someone's tooth. Let's go and watch!

When Humphry Davy and his friend came out of the fattest man's tent, they heard screaming and shouting.

In those days, dentists were not like they are today. Often they were really blacksmiths or barbers, not dentists. Crowds gathered to watch them work. **Pain-killers** had not been invented. Two people held each victim down while the dentist pulled.

They look like drunks.

Near the dentist was a tent. Its sign said, 'Laughing Gas. Try it. Laugh your head off for a penny.' Humphry Davy and his friend paid their money and went inside. A man let people lean over a bowl of liquid and breathe the fumes. As soon as people breathed the laughing gas, they started giggling. The tent was full of people laughing and staggering about.

But have you noticed something? When they fall over or knock themselves, they don't seem to feel any pain. That gives me an idea.

Next day at work, Humphry Davy began doing experiments. He breathed all kinds of gases. Each time, he wrote down what he felt. The work was dangerous. He had to be very careful with his experiments.

Some gases made him feel sick.

Others gave him a headache.

If I take more of that, I'll kill myself.

One knocked him out for five minutes.

It works, Laughing gas does kill pain.

The laughing gas from the fair was nitrous oxide. When Humphry breathed it, he felt light-headed. He pricked his hand with a pin and felt nothing.

Humphry Davy wrote a book about his experiments. He said that nitrous oxide, or laughing gas, killed pain. If people breathed it, they would feel no pain. At first, no one believed him. But then a dentist called William Clark gave the gas to a brave patient and was able to pull her teeth without hurting her.

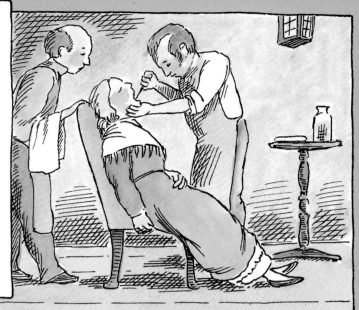

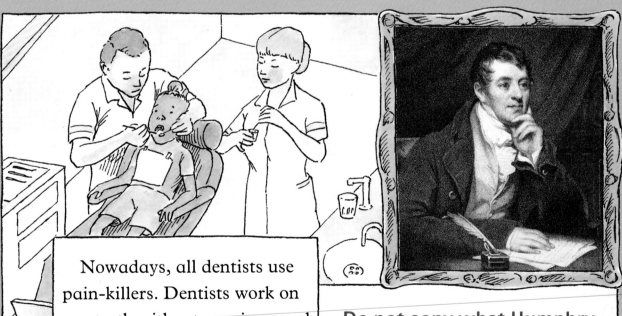

Nowadays, all dentists use pain-killers. Dentists work on our teeth without causing much pain at all. And it started 200 years ago, with Humphry Davy's idea about laughing gas, and his careful, thoughtful work.

Do not copy what Humphry Davy did. His work was very dangerous, but he had other scientists to help him. Never smell or sniff strange gases – they could make you very ill.

Skin

A skin-tight fit

We all have a suit of skin which covers us from head to toe. Your skin is perfect for you. Would it fit anyone else?

It is snug-fitting and strong enough to stop germs getting into our bodies. There are oil glands under the surface of the skin which keep it moist and soft. Skin keeps the rain out too because it is waterproof!

Touch

There are bundles of nerves in our skin. These give us our sense of touch.

Our skin tells us if things are hot, cold, rough or smooth.

Skin is thickest on your palms and soles of your feet. It is thinnest on your eyelids.

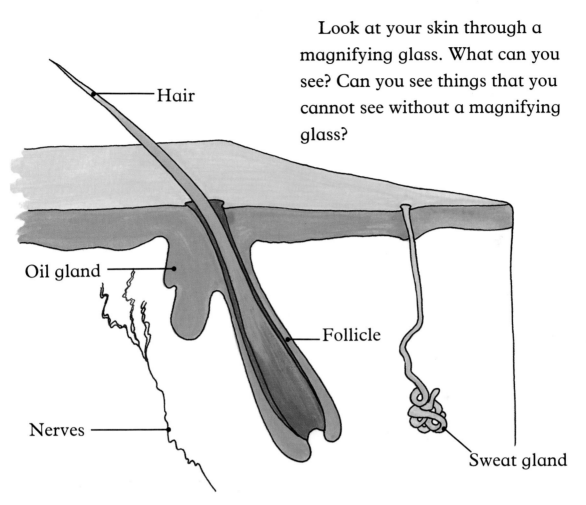

Look at your skin through a magnifying glass. What can you see? Can you see things that you cannot see without a magnifying glass?

Hair

Oil gland

Follicle

Nerves

Sweat gland

Diagram that shows what is underneath the surface of the skin

Keeping clean

Skin grows from the inside. The outside layer is dead. It is like a cover of overlapping tiles. Dirt collects here and bacteria grow. We must wash our bodies often to get rid of the dirt, dead skin and germs.

If you were covered with a metal like steel, it would last a few years and then wear out. Because your skin keeps on growing, it will last you for life.

Body temperature

Our skin helps us stay at the right temperature. When we are too hot, we lose heat by sweating water through our sweat glands. When we are cold, little muscles pull up the hairs in our skin. The hairs trap heat on the skin. We call this having **goose-pimples**. Look closely next time you shiver. Each little bump has a hair.

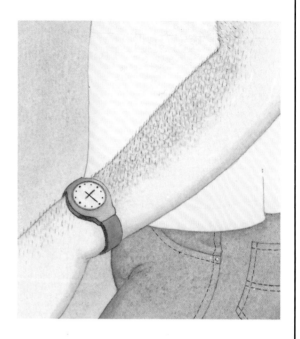

A sweaty marathon runner

An adult loses about a third of a litre of sweat a day. In hot weather an adult can sweat as much as two and a quarter litres a day – that would fill four pint milk bottles! That's why we have to drink more in hot weather.

Hair

Our bodies are covered with fine hairs. We lose most heat from the tops of our heads so we have lots of hair here. We have about 100 000 hairs on our scalp. This helps keep us warm.

Our hair grows all the time. It grows about 12 to 13 centimetres a year. It stops when it reaches our own special hair length. We lose about 50 hairs a day and new ones grow in their place.

Short hair

Long hair

Curly or straight?

Hair grows from tiny holes in the skin called **follicles**. Have you wondered why some people have straight hair and others have curly hair? It is the shape of the follicle which gives us our natural hairstyle.

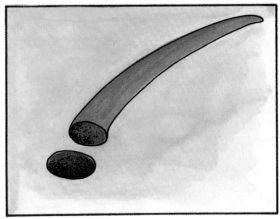

If the follicle is round, our hair grows straight.

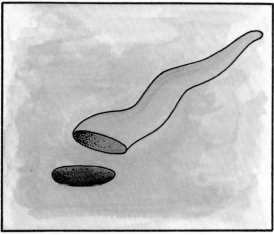

If it is oval, we have wavy hair.

Really curly hair grows from rectangular follicles.

What colour is your hair? Is each hair the same colour? Sometimes it is hard to say exactly what colour your hair is. Make a record of the hair colour of all the children in your class. What colour hair do most people have?

Animals' hair

Elephants live in a hot climate. Their skin is covered with tough hairs. Elephants need to stay cool. A good soak in a pool followed by a mud bath is just right. The mud dries on the skin and stops the elephant getting sunstroke.

Polar bears live in the cold Arctic region. They have bushy coats of fur to keep them warm. Polar bears eat fish and seals which they catch in the freezing sea. Their coats are so thick that their skin does not even get wet.

The Polar Bear

The Polar Bear is unaware
Of cold that cuts me through:
For why? He has a coat of hair.
I wish I had one too!

Hilaire Belloc

Identikit!

Make your own identikit set.

You will need some pieces of paper like this:

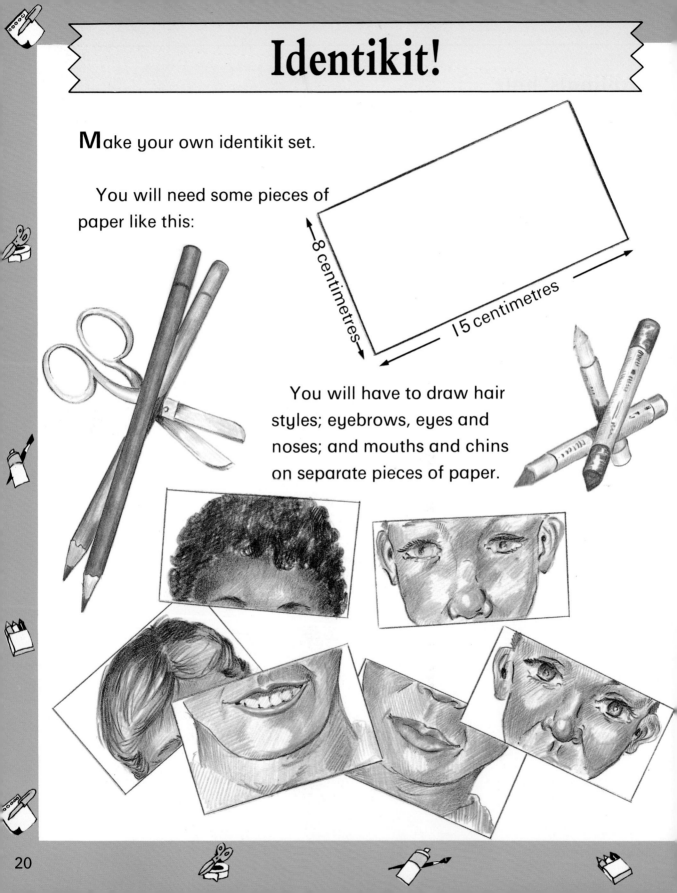

8 centimetres

15 centimetres

You will have to draw hair styles; eyebrows, eyes and noses; and mouths and chins on separate pieces of paper.

Look carefully at the people in your class. Draw as many different features as you can. You will have to think about these things:

Hair – colour and style
Eyes – shape, colour, glasses or no glasses
Nose – shape
Mouth – shape
Face – shape
Skin – colour and freckles

Identikit game

Play a game with six people. Five people write their names on scraps of paper and put them in a hat or container. The sixth person picks one name and looks at it secretly. The sixth person has to use the identikit set to make the face that belongs to the name.

The rest of the team then have to identify who it is.

Take it in turns. You can play this game at home or at school.

Nails

The nails on our toes and fingers are quite hard. Our finger-nails help us to pick things up. The little white half moons are where they are not firmly fixed to our skin.

Dirt and germs can collect under our nails. So we need to keep them clean by scrubbing them with a nail brush.

People who use keyboards in their jobs like typists and cashiers can work better with short nails. Piano players' nails must be kept short too, otherwise you can hear the sound of their finger-nails hitting the keys! Biting your nails can damage them and your skin, so try not to do it.

Finger-nails grow about four times faster than toe-nails. Can you think of a way to test if this is true?

Can you find out if the nails on your left hand grow more quickly or more slowly than the nails on your right hand?

Animals' nails

For many creatures, nails can be useful tools. Apes have hands shaped like our own. They can use their nails to scratch itchy parts on themselves and their friends. They will pick insects and salt off each other to keep clean.

⇑Cats need to keep their claws really sharp. They grip the ground with their back feet when they are ready to spring on to birds and mice. Their prey is trapped under their front claws. Cats' nails are so important that they can be tucked away. Feel a cat's paw when it is asleep. Look again when it is playing with a ball of paper. Do you know how cats keep their claws sharp?

Birds' claws are curved and pointed. They help them to grip on to branches, rocks and even the sides of houses. They can scratch places which are hard to reach like their heads and the back of their necks. The osprey uses its claws to snatch fish from the water. ⇓

Glossary

canines
The teeth at the side of the mouth which tear and shred food.

dentine
The soft layer inside a tooth underneath the enamel.

enamel
The very hard white layer on the outside of the tooth.

follicle
A tiny hole in the skin through which a hair grows.

goose-pimples
These are the small bumps that appear when we are cold. The hairs on our skin stand up and help to trap warmth near the skin.

incisors
The teeth at the front of the mouth that bite and cut food.

molars
These are the teeth at the back of the mouth which help to crush and grind the food.

pain-killers
Medicines which help people to stop feeling pain.

plaque
A sort of white fur that gathers on our teeth. We need to try to keep our teeth clear of plaque because it can damage them.

pulp
The part inside a tooth which contains blood vessels and nerves.

root
The root of a tooth helps the tooth sit firmly in the gum.